Mimic Pond

Also by Carol Watts

A Time of Eels (Oystercatcher, 2021)
Kelptown (Shearsman Books, 2020)
When Blue Light Falls (Shearsman Books, 2018)
Dockfield (Equipage, 2017)
56, a poem sequence (with George Szirtes, Arc Publications, 2016)
Many Weathers Wildly Comes (Spiralbound/Susakpress, 2015)
Flete, artist's book (2014)
Sundog (Veer Books, 2013)
Mother Blake (Equipage, 2012)
Occasionals (Reality Street, 2011)
'Zeta Landscape', in Harriet Tarlo, ed., *The Ground Aslant* (Shearsman Books, 2011)
this is red (Torque Press, 2009)
Wrack (Reality Street, 2007)
brass, running (Equipage, 2006)
alphabetise, artist's book (2005)

Mimic Pond

Carol Watts

Shearsman Books

First published in the United Kingdom in 2024 by
Shearsman Books
P.O. Box 4239
Swindon
SN3 9FN

Shearsman Books Ltd Registered Office
30–31 St. James Place, Mangotsfield, Bristol BS16 9JB
(*this address not for correspondence*)

www.shearsman.com

ISBN 978-1-84861-917-3

Copyright © Carol Watts, 2024

The right of Carol Watts to be identified as the author of this work has been asserted by her in accordance with the Copyrights, Designs and Patents Act of 1988.
All rights reserved.

ACKNOWLEDGEMENTS

Mimic Pond came together through an almost daily walking practice, begun in September 2021, with writing as a form of regular documenting taking place from January 2022 to May 2023. It carries some of the quiet attention that the pandemic brought with it. I'm grateful to many friends: Will Montgomery and Emmanuelle Waeckerlé, for their inspired *Walking in Air* project which gave me space to think and make at a walking pace; Harriet Tarlo, Tilla Brading and David Caddy for early pond encouragements; David Herd, Stephen Collis, Jeff Hilson, Iris Colomb, Agi Lehóczky and *Tears in the Fence* for the chance of readings; Peter Larkin, Jonathan Skinner and Katherine Zeltner for generous Midlands exchanges; Catherine Boyle for local wandering; Dave Watts for quantum pond conversations. John Kraniauskas has been walking across Blackheath with me for nearly thirty years, come sleet or sun.

POND

1

Dog Section / 11
Diaphragm / 16
Hollow / 22
Ear / 24
Palm / 30

2

Dog Days / 37
Bone / 42
Pulse / 49
Still / 53
Field / 56

3

Dog Star / 63
Fruitbody / 68
Glass / 73
Hole / 81
Figures / 85

4

Air-Dogs / 91
Sea / 97
Repair / 104
Glitch / 108
Mouths / 113

5

Dog Trot / 119

Afterword / 124

*Wild Notes,
Marginalia, and
Related Reading* / 126

for John K

here is a mimic sea – with its gulls.
        Henry David Thoreau, *Journal*, 16 April 1852

    infinity
so soon itself a limit
to objects forced into subdivision
as if words named themselves
        Tom Raworth, *Meadow*

The open world ... has no insides or outsides, only comings and goings. Such productive movements may generate formations, swellings, growths, protuberances and occurrences, but not objects.
        Tim Ingold, *Bindings against boundaries*

They are born otherwise.
They well up from the page.
        Francis Ponge, *The Making of the Pré*

One

Do not move stones.
—Sappho

Pond (Dog Section)

It was a wolf that led me to the heath.
Slinking, waiting at the turn.
I was grateful for its waiting.
I had seen it choose to get up on the couch.
I would visit nightly, to watch it settle
as if there was relief there
for its neuropathy or mine,
the difficulty of trust.
It would sleep & find a kind of peace,
enough to return to me in daylight dreaming.
Please come walking with me, I would say.
Now that you have found me.
It would walk just ahead, with narrow hips,
snaking mortally, like a dog.

The day is up!
We walk along a curve, tracing parabolas.
Slingshot around a pond's lip, sun at rest.
Rotating black holes might offer assistance,
but simple gravity affords us sight, here.
That unacknowledged shadow.
A black hole, its bright & spinning vortex
newly pinned by earthly telescopes,
revolves in space.
In January, the water reflects my movement
as we wheel, but not the wolf, who has a name
invisible except to itself.
Today only the dog section is mirrored in the pond,
fragments of lifting, bathing crows.

Dog section arrival seems a daily occurrence.
Folding over pond margins by the tea hut.
The crows raid the bins as if in provocation.
Lob it! Arrest us! Sometimes the dog unit
combines, framing reflection in police downtime.
Meanwhile water ripples and disappears.
I've seen how ponds can swallow mountains.
The presence of wolves. Also the extent of sky.
Relative to the movement of the solar system,
coronas of brass buttons, or memory of glaciers,
their ballast of stones & standing waters,
sea entering land, once looming distantly
over isles of dogs, at that time
when wolves became whales.

Wolf is apex predator on the heath.
What will you bring with your wildness? I ask .
The recovery of forests around this scratty pond?
Or watery metamorphoses, meanders through
these black beds, still laying their gravels down?
You have always been a child of gravels, it said.
Given to quarrying & percolations.
But remember the poet: *do not move stones*.
Infinitesimal monuments, scaling time.
A different order than walking in air.
So many seasons held in a rolling sphere.

Cut a door in the wolf so we can retrieve our dead:
another poet's maxim, I say.

For a world that matters.

I'm not that wolf.
Listen to the roaring of ponds.

Pond (Diaphragm)

Dry spring for a seasonal pond, earth's
diaphragm, a patch that weeps

now lush with clover & yellow flags.
Reeds stand in for water.

The stripping of a bed back to
cupped intention, small stones.

Always readying for return, as if by
upwelling.

Tensile accord with the way
weather runs, the sagging or rush

of air, slight moisture on skin, or
gorse blooms, pricked darker

red. Nothing is held here, porous to
deeper saturations,

black earth naming the place, its
levelling.

A blot condensing each day, drawing
it up, as if left by a down draft

next to the mound, its reversal into
open mouthing, or frame

dragged, slowing us down to
another extraction of

time's deposits, the chance of
voices.

A cairn of small stones appears, a child
cries *I didn't hurt her.*

Sits by the cairn unmoving, sound travelling
to an indistinct mother. April.

Now the stones have gone, returning to
smoother embedding, shards of glass

as if polished by seas, strewn
greenly.

To skim stones in this water you'd need
winter to return.

Storms are fat cells, rain falls in grey
skeins, unreplenishing.

To skim stones would be to send them
across space, twisting

a horizontal plumb line, pulled into radial
delinquencies.

Send them skimming, by this *mount
for trying mortars.*

History surfaces as ordnance, in
curious trajectories, flaring

as breath discovers barricades,
a boundary mark,

this pond: a diaphragm
for reverberating margins.

Pond (Hollow)

So, listen. A cup, auricular
hollow, settling to lips.

As if the world is a vast head,
resting sideways,

funnelling sound to deeper
anvils.

Imagine a head in its burial,
a maize god, set east-west

to grow with the sun, stony
hair waving like corn silk,

long as a cob, mouth
surfacing in the dirt.

Dreams breathe in & out
through reeds, their hollow

pipes, unseen, beneath water's
skin, for as long as

predatory searching goes on,
the world turning.

Beneath the mirror of a pond
its night galaxies, seeding new

mountains in brackish waters,
bitter waters,

star-starved, the head waits
to stir.

Whose is the head planted here?
Resting among stones, now

without water, reflecting
nothing of the sky, this flat plain

sat in the lap of seasons, wheels,
waits, hums.

Gravels work through burials
by a principle of extraction,

where ritual became exhausted years
past, crows remain with votaries,

scavenging gifts from the dead.
As the day sieves, it rises.

Pond (Ear)

Listen hard. Cooler under cloud.
To the absence of larks.

Above the leavings. Shells,
seeds, bones from domestic dogs.

Pot shards. Polystyrene puffs.
 A magpie feather with one white spot.

Bluish flints staring up wildly
in herd alarm, turn brown.

Mallard on the distant bench, becomes
a wine bottle on closer approach.

Its eyesight would be panoramic, continually
moving towards & away.

This ear, open to myopic resurgencies.
Hears the whole sky.

Sounds are tidal depositions, life
beyond petitioning.

In the evening the clatter
of may bugs, choosing

this time to live, whirring under
street lamps, as if desiccants

to the humid air, born of
buzzing rookworms, a patience.

Given to prognostics & trials. Cannoning
into midsummer.

Make collision the principle of
abandoned return, drone a word

for seeking lost trees, other
instars.

Shifting of may bugs returns a dryness
of remembered summers,

that accompanying beat of crickets
in the grass become straw, recalled

now in your skin, an older landlocked
living on ancient seas, reach of

outwash still drifting in me.
This pond's ear vibrates at the rim,

finds occasion for disappearances.
The hay *lain long hid* shines blonde,

lifts itself to the breeze, high rise
ragworts sway, watching for the

silences of butterflies, absent blocks
of air, as if sounding those deletions.

Is this a poor year, with so few to find.
Sounds of our lack denied

in the rush to flower, the fullness
of plants, unattended.

Heat arcs like a drum. Summer
brings velocities, beaks ajar, crows

spread wings close to the ground,
as if in full belly absorption

of deeper frequencies. That time of
explosion in our London yard.

Hawk. Taking out a slow
wood pigeon from above, then hunched

to tent what it had taken, eyes
unblinking, golden.

Is not the way of crows. Congregating,
without the pinpointing of descent.

They distribute severally, or hang in the air
revolving on loud contention,

sourcing black conglomerates
internal to the breeze, where lightest

principles of flight buoy momentary
uplift taffetas.

In May they mobbed a circus, tearing
holes in canvas, dropping stones

on windows, thwarted by the son
of a knife-thrower.

Finding excitements in gathering,
in their clamour a calling.

The pond is yellow as a threshing box.
The heath cracks there.

Crows have departed for Folly Pond,
raucous now in distant trees, shady water.

Here there is a listening to earth, its
ringing. As if the pond is resolving itself

into atoms, ground & air. Desertification
in miniature, like an inland sea

in a greater continent, where ships rust
on land drained of moisture, salt

sands drawn to the surface & gathering.
Hear the *host of marvels*, as if

condensing, *pouring from everywhere*,
abuzz & desiccate.

Pond (Palm)

Palm of my grandfather, rolling a fag, arrives with
scent of smoke. Over the river the marshes are up.
Pour on water, pour on water.
Fires spike.

A furnace man, maker of London bricks.
He loved the *inexhaustible mine* of language, how it
might keep him company by *dilapidated gantries*
each working day.

On a wet Monday in 1964, *a dash of mephitis* rising
from an adjacent dump, when *Automation &*
Computers seem as remote as the stars, he saw
how a brickyard altered

the choices of Gray's *Elegy*, & then later,
flights of *wheeling & banking* gulls, reminding
himself of Wordsworth's yellow primrose, how
it might be *nothing more.*

Shake that *nothing*. So the pond extends its ribbing,
a fleshy palm swollen in the heat, sweating its joints.
As our hands do, now we are given to time's
brittler calcifying.

Consider how ponds age without water.
Arid in July, brackish in earlier seasons.
Never reaching a full flush of accumulation,
as if scarcity is in a dance with land,

forgotten inventories & vacatings.
Pulsing over several hundred years, it sits.
Inverse to the mound, open cast,
tiers of worked exposure.

Those workings are weather made.
Ghosting manual hands, long buried &
smoothed away in denial of the carving of
canyons, the sore anxiety of sinkholes.

Living on a crust, above minings where
this watering hole pockmarks
long trails of extraction, pitted
by the carting of chalk & stones.

How gravels percolate histories of labour,
the construction of cities & distant palaces,
times of boom & commercial raiding,
the ravening up of basins, weighing

human ballast. No balance in
economic accountancies, in sands
& earth, setting everyone to work.
Find a living on manorial waste,

until land burrows back to its bed.
Deneholes surface, where chalk
bursts through anticlines. Subterranean
caves cut, large as dormant ballrooms.

Currencies of sand in trade-offs, aggregate
*black holes. Enough to build a planetary wall
27 metres high & 27 metres wide.*
Enough to swallow & make this city anew.

Heavier now than the mass of all living things.
So these ancient workings for farming (lime), for
seeing (glass), for building (bricks), part of one long
unacknowledged history now arriving participant

in full exhaustion. Sands pulled from the floors
of seas & estuaries, skimmed from dried lake beds,
changing the paths of rivers, shine in rising heat.
How we inhabit extraction, unspoken

as a birthright, leasing the ocean beds, eyeing
bright balls of manganese, blood cobalt.
This burning simplicity of stones.
Endless abstraction of aquifers.

Through every changeful year. Are we led
as before. Where the pathway ends in quarries,
silicate blooms *shadows of strange shape.*
Cut by rusty tracks.

Place of ghosts. Lines under a round red sun
conjuring late summer, berries staining skin.
Sheaves of bee orchids gone to ground.
Dryness etching time into sepia, the sere

in maternal memories suddenly younger
than my sixty years. Here the ground
rings like tin, has not seen rain for days, is
in dull compact with endings.

I love these lines, he wrote. *A primrose
on the river's brim.* But refused the man
in the poem, his *internal bait,* this violence
pitched toward clamorous nothings.

Two

Then had earth of earth earth enough.

—Anonymous fourteenth-century lyric,
Erthe upon Erthe

Pond (Dog Days)

It's hard to sleep.

Roamings of dog & wolf
in the early hours, still
sweating the light.

Retreat into night shade,
finding internal motion
to the beat of insomniac
hearts.

Shadows are a drought,
excavating granularities.

Wolf resting now in the fullness of day,
one eye open.

There's no walking together in this heat.

I'm no curative, says wolf.
You can't call me up.

They once took my right eye for insomnia
& my tongue for taxes.

There's extraction for you.

Now all the stones are rising
in the dry bed of the pond.

Plants creep low across the earth.
Reeds are rattles.

In Death Valley today,
a thousand-year flood.

Imagine the sun as a boat,
the liquidity of stones.

The heath has a millennial patience,
burning & sweating out its time.

A yellow truck parks up by the pond:
SWAIN.

Ah those bucolic dreams returning.
Delusional life, wolf yawns.

The heat draws it out like a fever.
I've nothing to counter it.

Go, walk.
Listen to the roaring of ponds.

Pond (Bone)

Tending to a sacral point,
a curvature stripped back to
tilt, a world's girdle.

As if we set out from
this arc of bone, learning
to walk again.

Taken to first principles,
a cupping & keeping.
Where gravity is grace,

it holds air, space, ground
in relation, so you can
walk a line.

Woken to others, again.
That's the point of bones,
their fluidity.

Scorched back to architecture,
finding all its forces newly upright,
in extension,

realigning. Nothing complex about
seeking balance, but the effort
to begin again.

This floor is full of stones.
There is nerve damage on the right side.
The ground is dark.

Yesterday the weather broke.
The rain arrived as if we could forget.
Water came down like a sheen.

Heath turned black beneath the straw,
true to its naming.
My neighbour heard

trees are more in jeopardy now
with the promise of water, than
when parched dry for weeks.

They begin to lose boughs.
As if the world is in amputation,
a harm now set in motion.

Thoreau. *In midsummer we are of the earth —
confounded with it, — & covered with
its dust.*

*From this offside of the year, this
imbricated slope, with alternating
burnished surfaces*

*& shady ledges, light & heat.
Now we begin to erect ourselves.
Somewhat.*

*& walk upon its surface. I am not
so much reminded of former years,
as of existence prior to years.*

Vision of an embryo today
discovered in dusty remains.
The earliest vertebrate.

Found north of Whitby, coiling
unrecognised in archives.
Ribs & flippers.

So waters break, & it slips
out of the museum, joining
schools of ichthyosaurs.

A novel sight for inland meadows,
birthed out of rock, like petrichor,
scent of stones meeting water.

Accompanied by thunderstorms,
a young mammoth is uncovered
in Eureka Creek.

She is on the land belonging to
Tr'ondëk Hwëch'in First Nation people
who name her Nun cho ga:

big animal baby. Geologists are pelted
with hailstones the size of golfballs
on taking her away, *as if*

*we'd released something more than
just the mammoth.* She is returned
to her resting ground.

Storms are a mazy release, returning us
to skies. Waters break, & the earth rests
in recovery, dry as bone.

*Aug. 18. A great drought now for several
weeks. Almost everywhere, if you dig
into the earth, you find it all dusty.*

Aug. 18. Waters break. A small girl,
named for the earth among all its colours
– bronze, andromeda, ochre, siena –

arrives in a time of heat & storms, the calm
of beginning. Takes hold of gravity
as a grace.

Pond (Pulse)

Life signs. Boom, boom, boom.
Base notes of a bank holiday fair.

Gain interior resound in walking.
Shake, shake, shake.

Mown hay sits up in peaks,
as if ridging by vibration.

Crows scuttle after insects,
tracking lines of intent.

A pulse. Throbbing sun,
then a night & day of torrents,

resolving into calm. Small scale erosions.
Soil mimics fractal tributaries.

Pond retains its empty reverb, fuzz
of green intimating waterless survival.

Nearby a struggling oak, loaded with galls.
Ink in tighter housings.

Fall in step, while your heart makes
counter beats by *Splash Mountain*.

While August gives out, answering &
resisting restless atmospheres.

In Sindh 67 inches of rain fall in one day.
Joined by glacial melt, floods overtopping

lives & houses. That line in Brecht.
When to speak of trees is almost a crime.

When to speak of ponds, is
barely a marginal good.

This meagre spot, lean to
aching seasons, captures time as

a fitful spirit level, its dry blister
punctured to air.

In the distance, neon lights,
humans flinging upwards.

Pond (Still)

The sheening sound of rain, unremembered,
meets a sudden counter force in recollection,

distributing like a memory held in skin,
as the enveloping of warmth might prove,

or the way dark rests in you at night,
the door gently knocking against its frame.

On the heath it sounds a sweating out
of soil & green, rye resurgent,

crows cockier, returning to the pond bed
a thimbleful of capacity

to distil light, a momentary puddle
catching at the sky, & afterwards retaining

all its bluster, the blue & the mounting shadows,
as if its own remembrance is on the move.

Wondering then if water's return to this place
is part of its alchemical swing with the year,

an alembic principle anticipating autumn – one part
dog star, two parts rain – stirred by bathing crows,

conning the sky. Last week walking to Rushy Pond
on another Black Heath – place of conjunction,

lost love & a wriggling moon – searching for
helixes of grass snakes in the water.

You'll see them in plain sight, she said.
One once found its way into his cradle.

What is it that swims from ponds into infant sleep,
into the making of poets, their mirrored days.

That pond was low & snakeless, agitated by fish.
As if flapping in failing oxygen, dark then light.

Here the water has vanished in a day, replaced
by greenest of shoots & leaves, spring madly

conjuring up from summer's ends, reeds
thrusting fresh, wild cabbage suddenly bold,

appearing from invisible repositories,
mixed from present air, saturated with

a queen's death & ancient monarchizing.
Watch the state turning to verbs & vowels

to remake itself again as nature. This place of
land-kings & rebellions, of scrub & litter,

silver whippits strewn in the grass.
Words float above the gatherings.

With bows & bills, with spear & shield.
On Black-heath they have picht their field.

Pond (Field)

What makes a pond more than field, earth of earth.

To another's eye, no pond but field.

No more than contour in air, its dry hollowing.

If a field carries potential for manifesting a force,

particles of objects inside it may change or move.

To think then of pond as a field of forces.

Pond particles that reassemble or move.

Holding birch trees in balance at the lip.

Say autumn ignites an assembling of this kind.

Now the equinox is done, mornings are quick & cool.

Nights clear to stars, or drawing in under cloud.

So heath swells a dark inflammation, thought laying down

intent in the expansion of spheres, a passing on of spores,

a slow abundant death, keeping pace *as the world asks.*

What does the pond hold, in abeyance, in its singular keeping?

As it ponds, a topographic low, cupping mist at first light.

Holds as a principle, while reeds return to ranks.

A curve catching at forms, dark weals across the field.

Bitter shadows, fungi spreading as stones in water,

tanning weathered shoes, rings bisected by paths

now left behind, the wind pushing fronts out east.

How they pool in thought of trespass, leaving marks.

Waterless place open to return, detritus of a year caught

constitutively, readying for decay, all the green tides.

All the leavings. Discarded CD, unplayable wheel.

Wa Ba Mi Gbe – Abide With Me in Yoruba –

rests on the pond's decline, as if glued by attraction

to congregant airs & pond assemblies, the swell

now seasonal & flocking, presses into field-work

almost drowned out with weeping & liquefaction,

as if power has a *slender marrow*, they said,

for a Tear is an Intellectual Thing.

Stony bed. Dry as an eye. Beads of rain.

Almost crystalline in suspensions. Tiny worlds

sheared in glass, as if pond agglomerates in

molecular visions seen from space, planetary

horizons shedding lachrymose returns.

Brackish truths condense in hungry times.

So this pond waits, is waiting.

Forces in a field, a gathering.

Three

how the smallest puddle
 reflects the entire sky
  —CAConrad, *Amanda Paradise*

Pond (Dog Star)

Passing over heads,
October scorches & burns
in all the colours.
Leaves flying spindles.
Warm plume from Africa.

Wolf trails pale as a moon rind
ranging in daylight.

A tail glimpsed among the crowds,
or loping, unconstrained.
There's purpose in pursuit of shadows.

Difficult to make you out
in all the noise, I say.
And you're up before dawn.

Wait for me?

There's a kite festival on the heath.

Sending up a distant cloud of flies.
Hanging as swamp mosquitoes do,
angular drones.

I imagine wolf as a grand dirigible, alongside
the levitating dragon & phoenix rising.

Buoyed up by air.

Typical, wolf mutters.
That you'd see me as a tethering.
Don't assume there's breath to go around.

It's a busy time, mixing with ghosts.
This uninterrupted stream.
Congregating in crowds.
Din of minor worlds.

What a hubbub!

*Sound of feet, a thousand times ten thousand
& thousands of thousands.*

On the heath they pitch their tents.

All souls.

Refugees & rebels, smiths & priests, hymn-singers, declaimers, petitioners, chartists, dockers, suffragettes.

Amend-alls. Delve & spin.

The dead singing *Wat Tyler went home too soon.*

This pond, subject to collisions where the land rises. Mouthless. *Clamor-filled shell.*

Earth. Sky. Justice. Power.
Living against living.

Stones, itinerant,
        resting on the edge of a name.

Feel the shock of future time, wolf says.

As the plants do.
As they move.

Water returning.

Walk.
Listen to the roaring of ponds.

Pond (Fruitbody)

Coming to the pond as a fruiting stage
in an ineffable cycle, spreading along
capillaries, extended by nerve nets
through rotations of time, as if place
carries connections continuously
chugging through the sugars, the dearth,
unknowable fungal contracts. Now
water is returning, the pond recovers
a familiar skin, tuned to sky & pocket
reflection, still retaining power to unsettle
human passers-by walking its stony
crucible, more beneath than captures
the light, as today – *oh no! marsh!* –
voices cracking, tramping the mire.

Water assumes clarity, oozes brown shallows,
rusting in a pact with days where plants
rise or fall, anchoring rosettes & tap roots
against the damage. Ribwort rat-tails, erect
as if in alarm, draw out metals, speak of repair.
Mats of knotgrass, sparrow tongued, are
peculiar against spitting of Blood. Or yarrow,
known as sanguinary, hardiest this summer,
flush with regrowth. Soft lush beds are
calvary clover, marked by spots of carmine.
This season of ghosts spatters ageing records
bleeding into the present, visions of a world
beyond *Conclusion*. Vegetal place of salving
& staunching, what *temerity* in mutual binding.

What measure in green apothecaries,
their stemming, their blood antidotes?
Naming the darkness in this black heath
drags up latent fantasies of blood & burial
from November air. The long survival of
a green plain, immiscible in its floating
beyond urban encroachments, seems more
than luck or resistance. Fears of dormancy
are local & explanatory, so pestilence courts
each & every story, all misapprehensions
& whispered lies. Who are buried here
among Cornishmen, armies & rebels, if not
numberless taken, victims of inflammatory
summoning. This pond, a plague apple.

Cleared ground. As if in a slow dying
listening to a world negotiating *discounts*.
The naturing of all capital contagions.
Gulls are falling from colonies in their
sickness, exposing bedrock beneath.
Too late to find refuge with the dead.
In Samoa the living reverence & oil
their bones, rescue ancestors from
ground, prey to brackish inundations.
Tell me you know water floods from
beneath, where our dust will settle.
I bring the pond home on my boots,
leave strands & sequences in return.
Spilt. You will find me scattered there.

A law to lock birds in their houses.
Starlings chatter uncontained, in
preternatural coilings releasing outside.
Flock, fall, bathe, pick as hens do, teeter
on street lamps, speak in wiry springs.
Geese fly over with morning, broken
lines heading east to waking estuaries.
Sparrows crash a commotion in bushes
by the Hare & Billet, exclamatory where
water is reliable. Crows. Across the heath
this flat glass folds into late sky, without
interruption, or stirring. Telling all that is
mirrored here under banks of pink cloud,
the mount emptying of ghosts.

Pond (Glass)

Enter this quiet fold in a moment, the pond
a replication of expanses

on different scales, wondering
what the pond sees in the crow

or the crow, as it flies, sees
in the pond

also in motion

Is it a seam for disturbances
as when she said

I think they know me, of the crows
she was feeding there

but then *perhaps they confuse me
with the man who comes each day*

to do the same

Or a placing of convergence
you might linger at

like the gutter of a book
that keeps things hidden

even as it opens to precise
proportions, or shapes to

an organising sky

In this way the pond appears
transparent,

a ponding faithful to its
own light, capture

differently rooted &
irreducible to

words

Yet words arrive, the drive to
predication annulled

as if strange to the making
of them here

alive to deeper verbs,
to the damage of realising

existences

As they refuse convergence,
as they are fitful,

like the word *impunity* which
rose here yesterday

when *glass* gave way to *well*,
& *well* to *hole*, a drawing out,

unannounced

Still in the saturated air, buffered
by mist, a counsel is kept.

Plants reserve their marks
at the surface, brittle, bending,

yield to drowned articulation,
or emerging mudlark

affordances

In the midst of who is hidden, who
begins again, an arc of struggle

swells to meet the air
which is water & light in depletion,

if not winter, returning a visible earth,
this hour, to its own

sentences.

Pond (Hole)

If *heaven is the impossibility of crows*
then this pond is their eden,

now elastic in the companionship
of rain, expanding like an eye

seen from above, low shafts of sun
catching at margins, tawny iris,

shiny watering hole for migration,
overflown, picked out in daylight

by gulls, now drumming on inland
earth, the first cries of refuge

from squalls & storms, or from
distant attrition, as if this green plain

might form a home from precarious
wanderings.

To think of this principle of refuge
huddled to itself.

Here we are in the dark. Muscular
retreat, flayed to delicate

exposures, how gold & pale,
flushed out hairless on

a planetary foreshore. The river
winds its wire beneath.

Seen from the sky, welding north &
south into a keen strip of light

you might follow. Once an edge,
along cliffs of ice. Here is shelter

already broken in upon. A place
you won't ever come to at night.

The man who sheltered here,
dug a hole four feet deep.

Tarpaulin for a roof. How many
years passed, unseen.

Years of his own midlife moulded
to shibboleths of gorse & crows.

His was concealment in plain sight.
No-one saw him come & go.

A refugee, in a brush thicket,
raised on a reed.

Sleeping among roots & stones,
a cold habiting.

That he did not give up. That he did
not give up, until the guns came.

On the south side of the heath, where
a church rises clean as a maquette,

there is, in certain reports, a fearful history
of vanishings.

An invisible glitch in spacetime,
given to curious deletions.

A flock of ducks in mid air. A child
kicking a ball. A highwayman in 1712.

A woman walking in sunlight. Dogs
& joggers subject to disappearances.

Think of portals & gateways. Then all
who inhabit the edge of sight.

Who disappear even as they are seen.
Brutal vanishments we live by.

Pond (Figures)

Now we sit at the fulcrum
of light & dark, sleepy with
solstice,

& have hatched from ice
this chance to tread time
its thickening

into pond shallows, caked
& uneven, opaque as
marble,

mottling with shadows, those
darker figures, testifying
to

the impossibility of fathoming
what has taken place
here

except a keeping faith
with shallows, not depth
or

anything further, yet rucked
as if with obscuring visions,
bottomless.

And the crows return hungrily,
floating & scrapping, hover
over

ice like black script, or old clothes,
torn & beautiful, suddenly
figures

on a page, as someone observed,
or notes on a stave, twisting
& curled

the way their wings shatter &
merge, like years
do

seeing ragged butterflies
alive in forest clearings,
floating,

recalled from shards of light
as if in intelligent adaptation
to a freak

of interleaving, the way wind
moved light along, there, &
nowhere else.

Here the light has glowered & gilded
its way through a cold snap,
forming birds

into figures surviving in the snow
against a pewter sun, against
removals

& fogs, dark illuminations cut
from breath & atmospheres,
the cold

scissoring them from seasons,
below the bright lines of
dusty meteors,

etching unseen all the debris
suddenly arriving at this
declination

as if weather lifts the universe,
shaking its dust while we sleep,
its sentinels

flocking to eat, & eat, fighting,
cawing, the infinite *so soon itself
a limit.*

Four

What if all ponds were shallow?
—Thoreau, 'The Pond in Winter'

in the great sink of being here
—Allen Fisher, *Black Pond*

Pond (Air-Dogs)

The year hangs
land into the pond.

Without decision.

Wolf is done with waiting,
setting off if I'm there or no.

It's no discipline. Keep up.

You loving wolf, I say, breathless.
Full of the dark light.

Water doesn't return you.

The day is up!

We retrace our tracks along generous parabolas.
Flattening pathways, wider & wider.

No sign of the dog section
parked up by the pond, not for months.

Perhaps you absorbed them.

Or sent them up feetless to float in thin air.
It's a tendency I've noticed, wolf says.

In you.

I'm trying.
Meeting gravity is painful.

How to find patience
to trust our heaviness?

You remember the poet.
*If we surrendered
to earth's intelligence
we could rise up rooted, like trees.*

Trees are on the move, wolf says.
They've never flourished here.
Ask the birches about their cozenage.
How they hang on by the pond.
Waiting for messages.

As for surrender.

If you could.

Wolf is already off around the curve.

The sky is mauve grey, winter cold, heavy with rain.
The pond has stretched across its bowl.
Thin as metal.

Words keep the floating steady.
I want to say.
Like gravel carted to Ballast Quay.

                           Stress, Stability, Draft & Trim.
                           Carbon equations.
                           Reeling us in.

All the stones.
I don't need many.

Sent along a line.

Attempting to keep the world light,
in balance, this pond

               open to casting, a shallowness
               in air & water.

Stone by stone.

It'll be thirty years before wolves return
to this mainland, I say. According to reports.

A recent cull in Sweden I don't pass on.
Bad faith smells rancid, it broadcasts like fear.
Wordlessly.

Like you'd let us in number.
You haven't got that long.

Walk.

Listen to the roaring of ponds.

Pond (Sea)

Here is a sea, an expanse
riffling in the air, responding to
currents.

Gulls have set up town halls across
the plain.

Beaching at news of greater inundations.

The moment a whale's eye breaches along a boat, sets up a rolling, while aligned, lazily.

That gaze is familiar, the way the pond looks up at the sky.

Rheumy with ice, or salt clear.

A mild & giving eye, one that returns the sea,
opaque light & ice-blink, as arctic
half-life.

Still reverberating under low cloud pollution,
so the day glows mutedly.

Grey snow light, as if under total eclipse.

All the norths are journeying, & the pond
for the duration of ice, retains this
echo.

Called to it, the heads of dark seals
rise from the surface.

Are rocks, hurled to break it.

Ice rears up in shards & fractures,
physics finds the push of time no longer
oceanic.

Splintering in feathers, or long lines shearing
like the Daugava, in remorseless rafting.

Pockets of trapped air.

Everywhere I step I make cracks! A child
stamps along the edge, where pockets
give way, popping.

The ice moans across its surface, the way tracks
telegraph the fast approach of trains.

Twanging electric wires.

When the melt begins, the pond turns dark
as ocean, & silent. A fantasy of depth,
unplumbed.

Something of a thickness. At night
this glassy aperture, under a clear sky.

There, a green comet.

Pond (Repair)

So the year stitches us in, & the pond
a watery blot, a blister, a lesion
nearer the heart.

Yet here comes the spring,
with its hopeful light, almost a gilding
in yellow thread.

I'm thinking of age outrunning tiredness.
The quilting of skin, a thinner parchment,
brings the world closer.

Say this transparency is to come, a pond
self, replenishing & then curdling
in air

over centuries, showing all the footfall,
dry dirt & gathering words.

There is a question of populations, bound
together, as when my grandmother took
many months over a pine cone,

sensitive to atmospheric pressure, woody
strands woven into tight stitched scales,
fraying on the wall of a cold room.

How that recall floats among the gulls today,
the smaller white ones, with black-tipped
wings, are hovering

on elastic strings, just above, at ease,
a stickier tide or stream in flow,
a layer denser near the earth, where

they breathe another climate,
looking down.

I try to remember the name of each stitch,
but names elude me, like small objects looking
back.

So an argonaut welds its paper shell, reflected
in the eyes of a seamstress who understood
living repair.

I try to think what repair lay in the pine cone.
The nature of her attention, something like mine.
Couching an enduring need.

Embroidered over & over, a daily presenting,
the fatter threads pulsing on the surface,
nearly held in place.

What a pond. A man walks by. A dog plunges in.
The other day there was nothing here at all.

Ah that *nothing*. How we are bound to it,
the way it moves & creeps, heavy
with cargoes.

And then binding in turn, our plunging in
& taking out, the anchoring, the running
& tenuous upholstery,

knitting, as in the tautness of a scar
dragging the skin, yet each stitch, each one,
a perforation

letting the world slip away, or push out straits
in small extrusions, bolts of lipid life, gradually
draining

as this pond shrinks, its edges darkening
& we wait for rain.

Pond (Glitch)

Predictions of another dry spring surface
in the calm of a barometric high,

cold taking over from the heat
internal to the sun's light, as if

you could have stretched & warmed
hands by it, only to watch it

founder.

The crows meet it too, massing severally,
their backs to the pond,

facing the sun, heads tilted upwards,
as if gazing at a distant atoll,

test dogs attending an atomic event
basking in its radiation,

tuning to heat.

Weather shapes us, still culturing in
nuclear proving grounds.

The force of five suns on movietone.
Toxic accords blocking out the glare,

islanders never to return, & us
growing whippy like sports, our father

of the H-bomb, which art. Etc.

Here is a glitch obliterating the spot.
Residual memory nosing out

radicles of *prodigious destruction*, those
murdering, mischief-doing engines

called bombs, already archaic but
falling now this European spring,

pierced to the root.

The pond is behind me. Without shade,
it listens to itself under a white sky.

The city growls & rings, baffled by snow,
already vanishing.

Slow hum standing in for silence. Arctic reach
in the wind, changes state,

skinlessly, while they fall.

Pond (Mouths)

Now the pond has entered my dreams.
Rocky percolations, folding into deeps,
spawn caves where water runs down
stony walls, mucosal vantage grounds.
Multiple mouths are creaturing into
worms & corals, amphibious fish-cats.
A gorgeous thermotropicalia stirs from
vents as if a wet market has been released
into freedom from caged menageries.
How life germinates! so you believe, sending
fingers toward future hours, while a night tide
is out & you spin over the cliff, zip-lining
into the air, joyful, the stubble below,
matted & mutable, mud & water.

There's a dream, an epiphytic wilding.
Daylit now, the pond ghosts me into March.
It's cold, goose-pricked. Larval.
Earth is heavy, mulched as if a herd
has watered there. Out east, houses
tumble from sandy cliffs, while a prehistoric
forest, exposed by lowest tides, stumps up
westwards. All on the move, careening through
unseen weathers, implacable equations.
We had a home, & then it fell. Once forest, now
stone & water. These live. Others founder.
A landlocked mouth, tied to time's clamour.
The yellow gorse is out today, its prick is real.
Hear bird insistences: *peet-peet, peet-peet*.

Dormancy begins to break, a calving
of counter earths. Listen for the roar.
The pond gives way to mouthings.
Go *wolfish swimming*. Water or no.
The best part of a day before you can see
the solid bottom. Put down bare feet.
Breathe this brown air, & in truth
your bones will grow thin, porous,
brittle as the days. But the wind picks up
& March buffets, your lungs are clean,
clouds trail streets across the water,
& the pond is electric with hatching.
A hole to see the sky through, mirroring
immensities, refulgent, a blue mouth.

Opening to speech & calling. *The very grain
of the air* is about to split. By the pond-shore,
an air-forge turns out sharp sweet rivets.
 A foundry full of moulds for casting.
Crows caw like organ pipes, launching bodies
forward. The breeze roils around, tossing
each thing, smoothing & disintegrate. Clouds
crackle, storm remnants build their banks, hail.
Do not move stones. These dark beds, laid down
in the rip-rap of epochs, in obdurate spring
under shallow seas & forest exhalations.
Worked by drought, ice, bird coinages.
Here they sit, readying to beach again.
A pond, mooring in air.

Five

Old John Hold used to walk up a streambed talking to it:
'So that's what you've been up to!'
—Gary Snyder, *The Practice of the Wild*

To note that mere 'existence' is already an upsurge
—David Abram, *Becoming Animal*

Pond (Dog Trot)

The clocks have moved forward.

Some confusion in corporeal time
brings me out ahead.

No sign of wolf, expectant treading
where the hill bends up. Click of claws.

Snaking mortally, like a dog.

So, walk.

There are tracks in the soft mud.
Green algae bubble in the water.
Reeds are bright toothpicks.

Someone is foraging on his knees under the gorse.
His mother watches him from her wheelchair.
Gathering the leaves.

Are you gone?

I walk along a curve, tracing parabolas.

At this winter's end, tracks become the widest hoop.
They merge into roads of deliberate intention.
As if we have walked in common, despite.

Crows are raiding bins, drawn by greasy leavings.
They barely avoid my feet on the path.
Holding their line.
                          All the small resistances.

One is taking the time to gather twigs.
Eyes averted, met in the moment. Nesting.

                   That first secret relay.

Two men are flying a drone from the mount.
I hear its whine before they come into focus, as it hangs in the air.

There's my shadow. It trails in the water,
                          seen from above.

Cut a door in the wolf.

Something holds true in its vanishing.
This biotic spell.

Binding seasons to earth's meniscus, here, to swellings & disappearances,
swallowings of vastness. Shallow reprisals. Dearth.

Levellings. *Wo was thanne.*

Tidal tails.

Caught translucent, treading timelapsed margins along an edge,
looping where there is sometimes reflection & spawning.
Wriggling faster towards future hours.

Soon the pond will become more of a nothing.
A dry lip in the black earth.

Will it be lost to me, then.
Say who belongs among the gravels, outwash, if not me.

Outlivings. Out lived.

Say, who.

April. The sun bursts land into tender, greener light.

Energy rampages in air, connecting luminous flesh, wings, drawing plants up from cold *mother-roots*.

A circus has pitched on the heath.
Come see nomads from the Mongolian steppes!
The Globe of Death! Aerial extravaganzas!
Its tent is captured in the water, among piebald clouds.

The pond is beginning to gather a surround.

Listen. Under day traffic, contrails, planetary hum.

Stillness.

How it roars.

Afterword

Mounts Pond is a small urban pond on Blackheath, the large grass plain above Greenwich in south-east London, named for its dark earth. It is one of four ponds on the heath – including Folly Pond, the Hare and Billet Pond, and the Prince of Wales Pond – the only one which comes and goes with seasonal weather. Records suggest it has been there for centuries, sitting by the old drover and carriage routes into Kent, the Shooter's Hill Road and Old Dover Roads, at what was once a crossroads. It can be found on Goffers Road, just along from the Blackheath Tea Hut. The land here is manorial waste, once frequented by highwaymen and excavated for gravels, now managed by Lewisham council.

The pond is named after the small mound which rises like a tumulus beside it, the only rising on this levelled ground. It is a place famous for rebellions, political speeches, assemblies and sermons. Currently it is known as Whitfield's or Whitefield's Mount, named after the Methodist preacher George Whitefield, who held open air gatherings there in the eighteenth century, preaching to thousands. It was the meeting place for Chartists and Suffragettes, who knew the earlier history, most famously the events of 1381, the Great Rising or Peasants' Revolt, when Kentish rebels led by Wat Tyler massed on the heath. John Ball reputedly made his famous speech – *When Adam delved and Eve span, who was then the gentleman?* – from this spot. At one point it was known as the Smith's Forge, after Michael An Gof, a blacksmith, one of the leaders of the Cornish rebellion in 1497 which rallied on the heath. It may be where many of the rebels were buried. Wandering through Kent in 1570, a historian recorded that it was still possible to see the place of the 'Smithy's tent', perhaps a burial mound resembling a barrow, he considered, of which there are a number in the area. Later the mound was used as target practice for 'those murderous, mischief-doing engines called bombs', as the local diarist John Evelyn, son of a gunpowder contractor, reported in 1687.

The pond sits in a surround which continues to carry these histories and related imaginaries in its cup. It swells and wanes with the season. Sometimes passers-by are unaware there is a pond there at all. In 2022 the water dried up by late April, and a dry, hot summer followed where temperatures exceeded 40° for the first time, with marshes and houses out to the east of London on fire. The water came again in late October, and persisted through to early June of 2023. As I write a year on in October 2023, following the rain of Storm Babet, the water has begun to return once more. The pond is a barometer of the climate, and also a neighbourhood shared with the rhythms of crows and starlings, humans and plants. Visiting has given way to deeper ties, and a common inhabiting of a precious, woven kind. The pond is fragile and sometimes vandalised, occasionally rubbish strewn, a quilting point on the heath that speaks to depletion and survival, yet open to endlessly attuning, shifting, sometimes spectacular light, and mimic proposals.

Mimic Pond is part of a practice of ongoing documenting, which is my living here in this neighbourhood. 'Born otherwise' in Ponge's words, the pond wells up and vanishes in these poems, and elsewhere in notebooks, photographs and a wider making.

Wild Notes, Marginalia, Related Reading

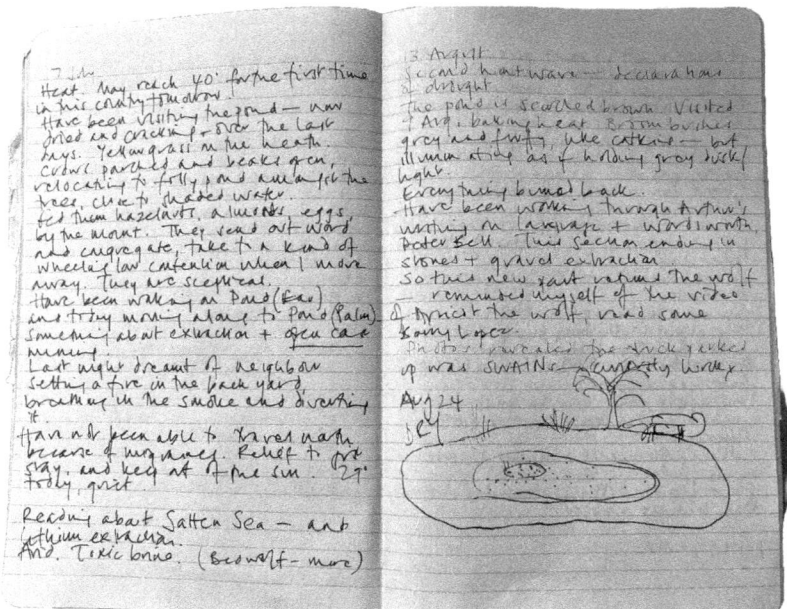

Epigraphs

'here is a mimic sea – with its gulls'. Henry David Thoreau, *Journal*, 16 April 1852.

'infinity/so soon itself a limit/to objects forced into subdivision/as if words named themselves', Tom Raworth, *Meadow* (Sausalito: Post Apollo Press, 1999), pp.21-2.

'The open world … has no insides or outsides, only comings and goings. Such productive movements may generate formations, swellings, growths, protuberances and occurrences, but not objects'. Tim Ingold, 'Bindings against boundaries: entanglements of life in an open world', *Environment and Planning* 40 (2008), p.1801.

'They are born otherwise./ They well up from the page'. Francis Ponge, *The Making of the Pré*, translated by Lee Fahnestock (Columbia and London: University of Missouri Press, 1979), p.215. My thanks to Peter Larkin.

Image: pond bed, with knotgrass and Blackheath gravels, 15 October 2022.

One

'do not move stones', Sappho, translated by Anne Carson in *If Not, Winter: Fragments of Sappho* (London: Virago, 2003), p. 293.

Pond (Dog Section)

Photograph of a black hole and its shadow, 6.5 billion times the mass of the sun, see https://www.nasa.gov/mission_pages/chandra/news/black-hole-image-makes-history 10 April 2019.

'cut a door in the wolf/ so we can retrieve our dead for/ a world that matters', from CAConrad's poem 'Camisado', in *Amanda Paradise: Resurrect Extinct Vibration* (Seattle and New York: Wave Books, 2021), p.20.

Image: looking towards the Mount, 19 May 2022.

Pond (Diaphragm)

'mount for trying mortars', located on a map by Samuel Travers, *A Survey of the King's lordship or manor of East Greenwich* (1695).

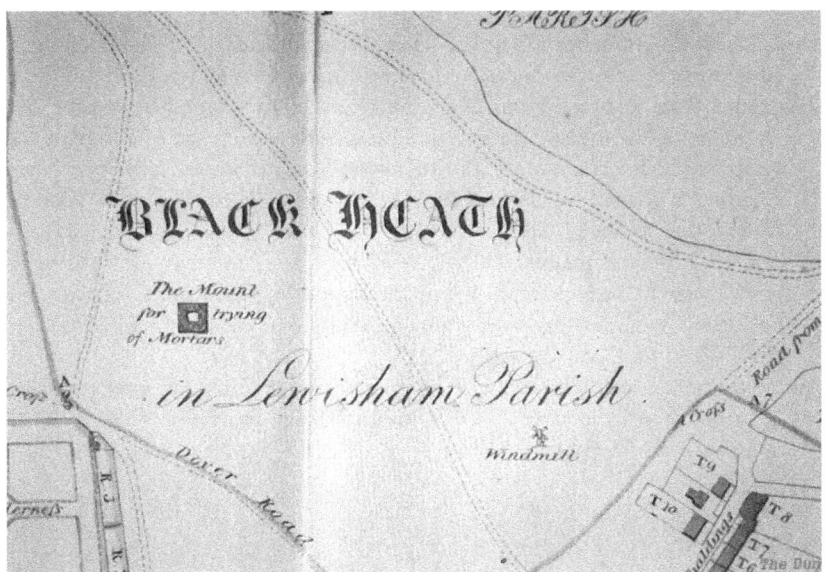

Pond (Hollow)

Discovery of the severed head of a Mayan maize god by archaeologists this month (June 2022) in Palenque, buried in a sealed box in a pond, dated from 700–850 AD. Mayans believed that ponds were portals to the underworld and mirrors to the sky. Mayan creation myths attached to brackish ponds or seawater, out of which mountains emerged.

Pond (Ear)

Eva Hesse, *An Ear in a Pond* (1965): 'Don't ask what a work is. See what it does'.
'lain long hid … lifts itself to the breeze', and 'host of marvels … pouring from everywhere', fragments from John Gower's response to the 1381 uprising, *Vox Clamantis*. Gower represents the rebels as clamorous animals, Wat Tyler as a grackle, like a crow or jay, 'taught in the art of speaking'. In his dream poem the movement of sea sand is a metaphor for gathering rebellion. Gower's works are online at The Gower Project Translation.

Pond (Palm)

https://news.sky.com/story/major-incident-declared-across-london-after-huge-surge-in-fires-and-homes-destroyed-on-uks-hottest-ever-day-12655061
Fragments from Arthur Watts, who read poetry throughout his working life, 'Introducing Changes: A report of a Week-end Conference of Foremen and Shop Stewards organised by the Industrial Welfare Society', *Phorpres News: London Brick Company Limited* 29:5 (May, 1964); 'Words – With or Without Music', unpublished (1964).
'Enough to build a planetary wall 27 metres high & 27 metres wide': https://www.theguardian.com/environment/2022/apr/26/50bn-tonnes-of-sand-and-gravel-extracted-each-year-finds-un-study. See also the documentary, *Sand Wars*, dir. Denis Delestrac (2013).
'nothing more', 'through every changeful year', 'shadows of strange shape' 'a primrose on the river's brim', 'internal bait', fragments from William Wordsworth's *Peter Bell – A Tale*.

Two

Anonymous fourteenth-century lyric, 'Erthe upon Erthe', which was included in prayerbooks before 1381. This version from fol. 59v of British Library, MS Harley 2253, taken from Susanna Fein, ed. and trans. with David Raybin and Jan Ziolkowski, *The Complete Harley 2253 Manuscript*, Volume 2 (Kalamazoo, MI:

Medieval Institute Publications), 2:96-97; and for wider useful context Marjorie Harrington's 'Of Earth You Were Made: Constructing the Bilingual Poem "Erþ" in British Library, MS Harley 913', *Florilegium* 31 (2014), 105-317.

> Erthe toc of erthe erthe wyth woh,
> erthe other erthe to the earthe droh,
> erthe leyde erthe in erthene throh,
> tho hevede erthe of erthe erthe ynoh.

> Earth took of earth earth with woe;
> Earth another earth to the earth drew;
> Earth laid earth in earthen trough:
> Then had earth of earth earth enough.

Pond (Dog Days)

Barry Lopez, *Of Wolves and Men* (New York: Scribner, 1978).
https://www.theguardian.com/us-news/2022/aug/10/death-valley-floods-climate-crisis
Image: looking from the Mount towards the bank holiday fair on Blackheath, 30 August 2022.

Pond (Bone)

Choreography of Klein technique, pelvic bone alignment. Thanks to Kate Johnson.
'In midsummer we are of the earth … existence prior to years', Thoreau, *Journal*, 7 Aug 1854.
https://www.theguardian.com/science/2022/aug/15/expert-makes-rare-find-sheffield-museum-opening-day-yorkshire-natural-history-museum
'a novel sight for inland meadows', Thoreau, *Journal*, 16 April 1852.
https://www.theguardian.com/lifeandstyle/2022/aug/19/experience-i-unearthed-a-mammoth-from-the-ice-age
'Aug. 18. A great drought now for several weeks… dusty'. Thoreau, *Journal*, 18 August 1854. *Walden* was published during this period of drought on 9 August.

Pond (Pulse)

'When to speak of trees is almost a crime', Bertolt Brecht, 'To Posterity'.

Pond (Still)

'conning the sky', Thomas Hardy, 'At Rushy-Pond'.
'With bows & bills, with spear & shield/ On Black-heath they have picht their field', from *The Rebellion of Wat Tyler, Jack Straw and Others Against King Richard the Second*, a ballad published in *The Garland of Delight*, 1612.

Pond (Field)

P. Steven Petersen, *The Quantum Tai Chi*, quoted by Pauline Oliveros in her *Quantum Listening* (ignota.org, 2022), p.53.
'Worchyng and wandryng as the worlde asketh', Langland, Prologue, *Piers Plowman*.
'Almost drowned out with tears', Life of George Whitefield: 'Prince of Pulpit Orators': https://archive.org/stream/lifeofgeorgewhit00billuoft/lifeofgeorgewhit00billuoft_djvu.txt
'For A Tear is an Intellectual Thing', William Blake, 'The Grey Monk'.
Drawing on Ovid's *Metamorphosis* and the stories of the protesting and grieving water nymphs Cyane and Canens who dissolve into the earth.
See Rose-Lynn Fisher, *The Topography of Tears* (New York: Bellvue Literary Press, 2017).

THREE

'how the smallest puddle/ reflects the entire sky', 'Camisado', CAConrad, *Amanda Paradise*, p.20.

Pond (Dog Star)

'Passing over heads': movements of the Dog Star Sirius were connected in antiquity to the dog days of summer, and to times of plague and their passing. 'When the piercing power and sultry heat of the sun abate, and almighty Zeus sends the autumn rains, and men's flesh comes to feel far easier – for then the Star Sirius passes over the heads of men, who are born to misery, only a little while by day and takes greater share of night.' Hesiod, *Works and Days*.
'Sound of feet, a thousand times ten thousand & thousands of thousands', Olive Schreiner, *Dreams* (1890), drawing on *The Book of Revelation*.
'Refugees': Blackheath's connection with refugees includes the thousands of impoverished Palatine arrivals who were put up in army tents there in 1709, a spectacle to visitors: 'What freak brought these poor creatures hither, is not easy to guess'.
'Amend-alls': Jack Cade's popular rebellion in 1450 massed on Blackheath with a list of bills of complaint on behalf of the commons – the first rebellion with

publicized, written grievances, a manifesto. Cade was known by some as John Amend-all, as John Stowe reported in his *The Annales or General Chronicles of England*, though the 'Mend-all' figure crops up elsewhere, not least in shaping the character of Robin Hood, emerging in ballads at this time. See Alexander L. Kaufman's *The Jack Cade Rebellion of 1450: A Sourcebook*, for documents.

'Wat Tyler went home too soon': 'Wat Tyler and his men were defeated by fraud. They went home too soon. We women must continue to demonstrate until the charter of our freedom is on the statute book'. Christabel Pankhurst on the Mount, to a crowd of 30,000, in 1912. From the excellent local history blog, *Running Past: South East London on Foot* https://runner500.wordpress.com/2018/11/28/suffragette-city-blackheath/

'Words are clamor-filled shells', Gaston Bachelard, *The Poetics of Space* (London: Penguin, 2014), trans. Maria Jolas, p.196.

Image: looking towards Hare and Billet Road, 23 October 2022.

Pond (Fruitbody)

Blackheath is often mistakenly associated with the plague, as if named for the Black Death, a persistent local fantasy. Perhaps because imagined plague burials could better explain the mystery of why the land was never built on than the intricacies of land ownership.

'peculiar against spitting of Blood': William Salmon, *Botanologia, The English Herbal* (1710).

'Conclusion': Emily Dickinson, 'This World is not Conclusion/ A Species stands beyond'. Dickinson wrote on the 'temerity' of the calvary clover plant, with its spots of blood.

'a slow dying trapped in a world negotiating discounts': Camus, *The Plague*: 'Think what it must be like for a dying man, trapped behind hundreds of walls ... while the whole population, sitting in cafes or handing on the telephone, is discussing ... discounts'. See also Samuel Weber, *Preexisting Conditions: Recounting the Plague* (New York: Zone Books, 2022), for reflections on the pandemic and narrating plague stories.

Gulls falling from colonies:

https://www.nationalgeographic.co.uk/environment-and-conservation/2022/09/the-uks-largest-avian-flu-outbreak-has-left-millions-of-birds-dead-and-scientists-extremely-concerned

Samoa: https://www.theguardian.com/world/2022/nov/04/the-climate-crisis-threatens-to-rob-us-not-just-of-our-living-but-also-of-our-dead

Pond (Hole)

'heaven is the impossibility of crows', Franz Kafka, *Zurau Aphorisms*, no 32.
raised 'on a reed', Charles Olson, 'In Cold Hell, in Thicket'.

https://www.newsshopper.co.uk/news/9600868.mystery-man-living-in-blackheath-hole/
https://www.mirror.co.uk/news/uk-news/homeless-mole-man-who-lived-771709
https://portalsoflondon.com/2017/09/03/a-door-to-nowhere-the-blackheath-vanishments/

Pond (Figures)

'Mottled intentionally by dark figures', Thoreau, 'The Pond in Winter', *Walden, Or, Life in the Woods*.
'so soon itself a limit', Tom Raworth, *Meadow*.

FOUR

'What if all ponds were shallow?', Thoreau, 'The Pond in Winter'.
'in the great sink of being here', Allen Fisher, 'Black Pond Scrap 6', *The World Speaking Back to Denise Riley* (Norwich: Boiler House Press, 2018), p.9. For more on the *Black Pond* work, see https://allenfisher.co.uk/writing/

Pond (Air-Dogs)

'Air-dogs', see Kafka, *Investigations of a Dog* (London: Penguin, 2018), trans. Michael Hofmann.
'The land into the lake', Friedrich Hölderlin, 'Half of Life', *Poems and Fragments* (London: Anvil, 2004), trans. Michael Hamburger, p. 461.
'Full of the dark light', 'Remembrance', Hölderlin, trans Hamburger, p.577.
'patiently to trust our heaviness', 'If we surrendered… like trees': Rainer Maria Rilke, 'Gravity's Law'.
'stress, stability, draft and trim': https://bulkcarrierguide.com/ballast-handling.html

Image: looking towards Shooter's Hill Road and the Blackheath Tea Hut, 17 December 2022.

Pond (Repair)

https://www.sciencefriday.com/articles/the-seamstress-and-the-secrets-of-the-argonaut-shell/

Pond (Glitch)

'test dogs': https://www.orau.org/health-physics-museum/collection/nuclear-weapons/weapons/atomic-goggles.html

'I saw a trial of those devilish, murdering, mischief-doing engines called bombs, shot out of a mortar-piece on Blackheath. The distance that they are cast, the destruction [which] they make where they fall, is prodigious.' John Evelyn in his diary, 1687.

At the time of writing the war in Ukraine has entered its second year.

Pond (Mouths)

The Lendbreen ice patch in Norway is giving up its objects as the climate warms.

Frieda Kahlo, *Lo que el agua me dio* (1938), translated as *What the Water Gave Me* or sometimes *What I Saw in the Water*.

Beowulf, translated by Seamus Heaney, p. 49. Beowulf dives into the water of a mere and 'It was the best part of day/before he could see the solid bottom'. Grendel's mother, who lives there, is described as a 'wolfish swimmer'. For the figurative limits of the mere, and its connection to a lake that foretells the future by its roar, see Richard Butts, 'The Analogical Mere: Landscape and Terror in *Beowulf*,' *English Studies* 68 (1987), p.118.

Thoreau, *Journal*, February 18 1857: '*The very grain of the air* seems to have undergone change and is ready to split into the form of the bluebirds' warble… the air over these fields is *a foundry full of moulds for casting.*'

Thoreau, *Journal*, February 20 1857: 'If I were to discover that a certain kind of stone by the *pond-shore* was affected, say partially disintegrated, by a particular natural sound, as of a bird or insect, I see that one could not be completely described without describing the other'.

Pond (Dog Trot)

'Old John Hold used to walk up a streambed talking to it: "So that's what you've been up to!"' Gary Snyder, *The Practice of the Wild*, (Berkeley, CA: Counterpoint, 1990), p.49.

'To note that mere "existence" is already an upsurge', David Abram, *Becoming Animal: An Earthly Cosmology*, (New York: Vintage, 2011), p.49.

'Wo was thanne': John Ball, 'When Adam dalf, and Eve span/ Wo was thanne a gentilman?' Sermon given on Blackheath reportedly to 'two hundred thousand of the commons'. For documents see Richard Barrie Dobson, *The Peasants' Revolt of 1381* (London: Macmillan, 1970), p.374.

'mother-root', George Herbert, 'The Flower'.

Image: looking towards the Mount, 25 March 2023.

Afterword

William Lambarde, *A Perambulation of Kent: Conteining the Description, Hysterie and Customes of that Shyre* (London, 1570), later edition of 1596, p. 434. https://www.durobrivis.net/library/1596-lambard.pdf

Image: pond from the Mount, looking towards Shooter's Hill, 28 November 2023.

www.ingramcontent.com/pod-product-compliance
Lightning Source LLC
Chambersburg PA
CBHW031633160426
43196CB00006B/401